To Mummy and Daddy.
from Walter
Christmas 1941.

M CAIRNCROSS.
P.O. HOUSE
KINNESSWOOD
KY13 7HN

One Hundred Details
from Pictures in the
National Gallery

One Hundred
DETAILS
from Pictures in the
NATIONAL GALLERY

With an Introduction and Notes by
KENNETH CLARK

1938
Printed for the Trustees
LONDON

PRINTED BY HARRISON & SONS, LTD.,
PRINTERS TO HIS MAJESTY THE KING
44 TO 47, ST. MARTIN'S LANE, LONDON, W.C.2

INTRODUCTION

THIS book contains one hundred photographic reproductions of details taken from pictures in the National Gallery. They have been chosen chiefly for their beauty, and since two details must face one another when the book is opened, they have been arranged in such a way as to bring out certain analogies and contrasts. Some of these contrasts are like epigrammatic summaries of the history of art, in particular those at the beginning of the book, which show the differences between Northern and Mediterranean painting. But the majority of openings have been arranged because the details have something in common, either of movement and design or of subject and mood. Violent contrasts have been avoided lest they should destroy the beauty of the individual pictures; for the platitude that great works of art of any epoch always go well together is untrue. Great pictures grumble at each other, insult or even annihilate each other as often as great men.

As with any form of anthology, the choice must ultimately reflect the taste of the chooser, and this may be one reason why so many details are taken from Italian painting of the 15th and 16th centuries. But there is another reason, that pictures in a style based on firm delineation, a style requiring equal finish in all the parts, yield far better details than pictures in what may be called an impressionist style, where the degree of finish grows less as the eye moves away from the focal point.

Although almost all the details are beautiful in themselves, a few are chosen for historical or iconographical reasons, as for example Bassano's malicious portrait of the aged Titian (Plate 20); and a few others were included because they were so unexpected. Even those who know the Gallery well may not have noticed the quarrel between a bear and a lion in Filippino's *Madonna and Child* (Plate 65). The landscape in Plate 43 comes from one of the most familiar of all pictures, yet some people may fail to recognise it at the first glance. And how many will recall the source of Plate 10 or, for that matter, of Plate 54?

Our failure to recognise some of these details may provide an amusing game; it also has an important meaning. It means that we do not look at pictures carefully. There was much to be said for the old naïve method by which people read a picture like a book. We, in our anxiety to avoid a literary approach, are often content with a quick synthetic impression. It may be true that a work of art can be recognised in the first second, but this does not exhaust its potentialities. The great value of these photographic details is that they encourage us to look at pictures more attentively, and show us some of the rewards of patient scrutiny. They are, in fact, an aid to appreciation more valuable, because more concrete, than the numerous books on how to look at pictures. They fulfil one of the first functions of criticism by presenting familiar material from a fresh point of view. This is particularly true of large pictures when, for physical reasons alone, it is difficult to give equal attention to all the parts. Take Matteo di Giovanni's *Madonna of the Girdle*. We have all seen her head, but from a distance of about twelve feet, and the reproduction on Plate 36 reveals a firmness and simplicity of drawing which the most attentive gaze could not perceive from below. The angels which surround her are too numerous for us easily to appreciate their individual graces; in detail they provide some of the most beautiful pictures in the book (Plate 89). Another example is the distant landscape high up in Pollaiuolo's huge *Martyrdom of St. Sebastian*, which turns out to be worthy of a place opposite Rubens' *Château de Steen* (Plate 26).

Although the beauty of such details seems obvious to us, they had been taken for scientific purposes for many years before anyone thought of reproducing them for their own sakes; and I believe it was the Japanese critic, Yukio Yashiro, who first used them as aids to appreciation in his book on Botticelli. From a scientific point of view, full size photographs are often very misleading. We are so accustomed to making allowances for reduction of scale, that photographs the size of the original make anything but the most polished handling look rough. As a result, a painter such as Bronzino is flattered, whereas the details from Piero della Francesca's *Nativity* are so disappointing that none has been included. Nevertheless, many of the photographs in this book are almost the actual size of the original, and where reduction has been necessary it is indicated in the notes.

I have written a note to almost every plate or pair of plates. Some of these notes contain scraps of information or criticism which may interest students, but as a whole they are intended for the average reader. They represent the kind of conversation which two people fond of painting might have while going round the National Gallery. One good result of this informal method is that every note shows a different approach, for nothing is more fatal to criticism than the fallacy of one cause. Just as a great river does not flow from a single source, but is made up of innumerable tributaries great and small, so the total impression of a work of art is built up of a hundred different sensations, analogies, memories, thoughts—some obvious, many recondite, a few analysable, most beyond analysis. Faithfully to record, in front of concrete examples, whatever impressions the moment admits, suits the informal arrangement of the book as a whole, and allows me to set down certain ideas which might not otherwise find expression and which may start trains of thought in the reader's mind.

The merits of this book depend on the fine quality of the original photographs reproduced, all of which were taken by the Gallery staff. Mr. W. D. Booker, the founder of the Publications Department, had a high standard of technical achievement which has been admirably maintained since his retirement. My thanks are due to the Photographic Staff, in particular to Miss A. M. Rickeard ; and to Miss O. M. Cook, the Supervisor of Publications, who has edited the book and seen it through the press.

Notes

Plate 1. Nicholas of Tolentino's Page from THE ROUT OF SAN ROMANO (583) by PAOLO UCCELLO, painted about 1450–60. Scale reduced.

This beautiful head, the embodiment of youthful chivalry, should dispose of the idea that *The Rout of San Romano* is no more than a glorified nursery picture. It is not only one of the finest pieces of colour and design in the Gallery but shows that Uccello was capable of creating a world more vital than the classical painting of the next century and no less authentically ideal.

Plate 2. Jan Arnolfini from JAN ARNOLFINI AND HIS WIFE (186) by JAN VAN EYCK, painted in 1434.

Plate 3. St. Nicholas of Bari from THE ANSIDEI MADONNA (1171) by RAPHAEL, painted in 1506. Scale much reduced.

The book contains several contrasts between North and South, between the Gothic naturalism of Flemish painting and the scientific humanism of Italian ; but none more complete and essential than this. In the van Eyck the forms are thin and asymmetrical—the face under its disproportionate hat, the hand, the flame of the candle. In the Raphael they are large and geometrical. They obey the laws which man's intelligence has imposed on durable materials, in architecture or machinery. The Arnolfini is like a flower, developing its tissue according to the laws of natural growth. This dwelling on a substance for its own sake is extended to inorganic objects like the brass candlestick, whereas St. Nicholas's crozier is merely a generalised shape in the balance of the composition. I find that these details are complementary to one another. The van Eyck brings out the wonderful plastic sequences of the Raphael, but has a delicacy of perception both physical and spiritual, which Raphael has excluded.

Plate 4. Venus from MARS AND VENUS (915) by SANDRO BOTTICELLI, painted about 1485. Scale much reduced.

Plate 5. Jeanne de Chenany from JAN ARNOLFINI AND HIS WIFE (186) by JAN VAN EYCK, painted in 1434.

The confrontation of two such profoundly different pictures borders on sacrilege, but may, I hope, be forgiven for the clear and concentrated way in which it expresses two opposing pictorial ideals. Moreover, it supplements the comparison of Flemish and Italian painting attempted in the notes to Plates 2 and 3, 6 and 7, the points at issue being rather different. Should a painter create a new world of beauty out of his imagination ? Or should he content himself with painting what he sees and trust that beauty will grow out of the actual seeing and rendering ? These details show that he can do either, if in each case his vision is sufficiently coherent. It is tempting to say that the Botticelli is poetry, the van Eyck prose, but like most analogies between the arts it is untrue, for a painter's joy in the perception of light passing over a white cloth can only be called poetical.

Plate 6. St. Giles and the Wounded Deer from THE LEGEND OF ST. GILES (1419) by the MASTER OF ST. GILES, FRANCO - FLEMISH SCHOOL. painted about 1500. Scale reduced.

Plate 7. A Group of Archers from THE MARTYRDOM OF ST. SEBASTIAN (292) by ANTONIO POLLAIUOLO, painted in 1475. Scale much reduced.

The contrast between North and South, analysed in the notes to Plates 2 and 3, 4 and 5, can here be brought out by a mere description of the subjects. St. Giles is protecting a deer, wounded by an arrow which has pierced the saint's own hand. The huntsman, dressed in a voluminous cloak of velvet and brocade, kneels in expiation, surrounded by clusters of wild flowers—iris, hollyhock, wild strawberry, wood spurge, briar rose—all most lovingly drawn. Pollaiuolo discloses a very different world. No fuss about flowers, no pother about a wounded animal. Six magnificent ruffians are discharging their arrows at the naked, defenceless body of a young man. From the ethical point of view perhaps the Northern picture is preferable, but Pollaiuolo was not concerned with ethics. He was concerned with the science of picture-making in which, to the Florentine mind, the most important part was the rendering of movement and the most noble subject *un bel corpo ignudo*. His subject is merely a pretext for a play of muscle ; and in consequence we feel less sympathy for the tortured saint than for the wounded deer. On the contrary our sympathy is with the archers, whose magnificent vigour is invigorating to us. The two men in the foreground bending over their crossbows are one of the best examples in art of those ideated sensations which Mr. Berenson made the basis of his essay on Florentine Painting.

Plate 8. St. Catherine and Canon Richard de Capelle from THE MARRIAGE

OF ST. CATHERINE (1432) by GERARD DAVID, painted about 1505. Scale much reduced.

David is the interpreter of a bland, unruffled piety which the merchants of the Netherlands demanded of their painters, in reaction, perhaps, against the bleeding hearts, flagellated Christs and other violent emblems of popular religion which were common throughout the fifteenth century. " Above all, no enthusiasm " : it is the forced tranquillity which preludes a revolution. In less than twenty years Luther will have appeared on the scene and Richard de Capelle, with his well-ironed surplice over a fur coat, will have vanished, as Carlyle would say, into oblivion. Unfortunately for the theorists, however, this complacent bourgeoisie had inspired a great school of painting, while the succeeding period produced, with rolling and gnashing of teeth, fewer good works of art than any century since the Dark Ages.

Plate 9. From THE MASS OF ST. GILES (4681) by the MASTER OF ST. GILES, Franco - Flemish School, painted about 1500.

Apart from its beauty this picture is a most important archaeological document, for it contains representations of the lost treasures of St. Denis. These are described in old inventories, and we can see how accurately the painter has imitated the originals, only reducing their scale in relation to his figures. This detail shows the golden retable which had been presented to the Abbey by Charles the Bald in the ninth century, and was destroyed in the French Revolution.

Plate 10. A Child from THE ANNUNCIA-TION (799) by CARLO CRIVELLI, painted in 1486.

Plate 11. A View through a Window from THE VIRGIN AND CHILD WITH A FIRE-SCREEN (2609) by "CAMPIN," painted about 1430-35.

The small child from Crivelli's *Annunciation* looks round the corner of a balcony and sees through " Campin's " window a beautiful toy town, brighter and more real than anything she could have found in Italian painting of the time.

Plate 12. A Faun from THE DEATH OF PROCRIS (698) by PIERO DI COSIMO, painted about 1500.

Plate 13. A Satyr from PEACE AND WAR (46) by SIR PETER PAUL RUBENS, painted 1628-29.

After long banishment those hairy devils of the Middle Ages, the Satyrs, returned to a popularity greater than they had known in antiquity ; for in the Renaissance they were no longer part of a living superstition, and so no longer alarming. Archaeology tamed but did not convert them. They remained symbols of sensuality unobstructed by conscience, and it is not surprising to find them, in the portable form of bronzes by Riccio and his school, among the minor household gods of the sixteenth century. But they even survived the Counter Reformation, appearing in force round Amanati's fountain in the Piazza della Signoria ; and they populated the imaginative painting of the *seicento*, on Caracci's ceiling, in Poussin's Bacchanals and in the work of Rubens, who gives them their full, lusty force, and something of the country coarseness which was part of their original character. The distinction between Satyrs and Fauns, already lost in Roman literature, is hardly ever observed. Nearly all the Satyrs have goats' feet, and the Fauns have lost their divinity. But Piero di Cosimo, in his devoted reading of antique poetry, has

discovered the original Faun, the shy, half-human creature for which he had an especial tenderness. It was a conception too subtle and sentimental for the sixteenth century as a whole, but there is a Carracci drawing of a faun at Chatsworth which bears the inscription *non so se dio m'ajuta*, I do not know if God is helping me, and this is close enough to the spirit of Piero di Cosimo.

Plate 14. A Scoffer from THE CROWNING WITH THORNS (4744) by HIERONYMOUS BOSCH, painted about 1495.

Plate 15. St. Demetrius from THREE SAINTS (669) by L'ORTOLANO, painted about 1520. Scale much reduced.

The connexion between Hieronymous Bosch and that dreary Ferrarese, l'Ortolano, is unexpected, yet these heads go well enough together because both have an element of expressionism, a slight over-emphasis rare in Italian art. The detail of Bosch's Shakespearean clown shows the sensibility of touch which distinguishes his work from that of his imitators, past and present. The head of St. Demetrius must be far the most striking thing l'Ortolano ever did, and results from a judicious mixture of Roman and Venetian influences. The motive of the hand covering mouth and beard seems to have been invented by Leonardo in his sketches for the Uffizi *Adoration*, and thence borrowed by Raphael for the figure of St. Paul in his *St. Cecilia*. The eclectic Ortolano must have seen Raphael's altarpiece in the neighbouring town of Bologna and in this picture he has turned the figure round to face the spectator ; and he has added a romantic spirit deriving from Giorgione.

Plate 16. Musicians from THE TRIUMPH OF JULIUS CAESAR (278) by SIR PETER PAUL RUBENS, painted 1629-30.

Plate 17. Trumpeters from THE ROUT OF SAN ROMANO (583) by PAOLO UCCELLO, painted about 1450–60. Scale reduced.

The contrast in handling is too obvious for exposition, and is made more striking by the fact that Rubens is actually following, with considerable freedom, a Renaissance design.

Plate 18. A Dwarf from THE FAMILY OF DARIUS BEFORE ALEXANDER (294) by PAOLO VERONESE, painted about 1565. Scale much reduced.

Paolo Veronese must have been one of the first great painters to introduce figures into his pictures purely for their decorative or picturesque value, without regard to dramatic significance. In this he was the reverse of his great contemporary, Tintoretto, to whom the drama of the composition as a whole was all-important. As Veronese said himself, " If there is any space left over in a picture I adorn it with figures according to my invention." So there was a critical, as well as a religious meaning in the condemnation pronounced on him by the Inquisition in 1573 for putting " buffoons, drunkards, Germans and similar scurrilities " into his great picture of the Feast at the House of Levi. Paolo Veronese might have replied with the scholastic definition of art *quod visum placet*, for there was never a greater master of what pleases the eye. Actually he tried to defend himself by referring to the naked figures in Michelangelo's *Last Judgment*, and received a well-directed snub, for, as the Inquisitor said, in those figures there is nothing which is not spiritual —*in quelle figure non vi è cosa se non de spirito.*

Plate 19. A Group of Sabine Women from THE RAPE OF THE SABINES (38) by SIR PETER PAUL RUBENS, painted in 1635. Scale much reduced.

Rubens's love of life is so great that we do not stop to analyse his mastery of the technique of painting. In this composition the marvellous skill with which he has built up a series of rhythmic sequences—curves enclosed in contrasted diagonals, like fish in a net—is forgotten in our general sense of exhilaration. The whole group has the sparkle and buoyancy of the waves. To our eyes there is something rather charming in the lack of reluctance shown by most of the victims, and the way in which the older ladies urge any who are nervous to take the matter in the right spirit. But a hundred years ago the author of a guide to the Gallery, criticising Hazlitt's famous description of the picture as " plump, florid viragos struggling with bearded ruffians," says : " everyone knows that most women when thus rudely and suddenly assailed are florid with indignation."

Plate 20. An Elderly Money Changer from CHRIST DRIVING THE MONEY CHANGERS FROM THE TEMPLE (228) by JACOPO BASSANO, painted about 1565–70. Scale much reduced.

The old man is a portrait of Titian, notorious among his colleagues for his love of money. Bassano has even caricatured one of Titian's own self-portraits, now in the Kaiser Friedrich Museum, Berlin, adapting the pose to one who is trying to shield his possessions.

Plate 21. Pilate and the Jews from CHRIST BEFORE PILATE (1400) by REMBRANDT, painted in 1634.

Early Rembrandts are, on the whole, the ugliest pictures ever produced by a supremely great artist. Yet they show an uncompromising devotion to the truth which is most impressive. Rembrandt would not accept the second-hand imagery by which his contemporaries were content to render religious and historical subjects ; he would not allow himself the technical tricks by which they evaded difficulties of drawing. He would not deviate from the truth of his imagination. This stubborn integrity, so closely resembling that of the young Cézanne, led to crudities which are sometimes almost insupportable ; but even the worst of them have great dramatic force. In this detail, after the first shock has worn off, we become aware of the psychological skill with which the various types of pomposity, bestiality and hysteria are contrasted : Pilate, timid, commonplace, watery-eyed, is like the chairman of an unsuccessful company assailed by angry shareholders. And all these dramatic inventions are set down with an intensity which, for the moment, makes the conventions of more polite painting seem empty and insincere.

Plate 22. From THE WATERING PLACE (4815) by SIR PETER PAUL RUBENS, painted about 1625 (perhaps begun in 1615). Scale reduced.

Plate 23. From THE MADONNA OF THE MEADOW (599) by GIOVANNI BELLINI, painted about 1500.

These details provide the fullest measure of contrast in the book, and show that extraordinary change in the sense of space which characterises the transition from Renaissance to Baroque. Bellini thinks of space as something static, orderly and limited. His walls and palings, even his cows and goats, are parallel with the picture plane. For the most part they are horizontal, and these horizontals are set off by a series of beautifully spaced verticals, towers, posts, trees and the white-robed shepherd. Each

interval is calculated with a sense of finality, as if nature had crystallised at some moment of perfection, and would never again be disturbed. We are reminded of Seurat. Turn to Rubens and space has become dynamic. Everything is in movement—not random movement, but that surging, twisting rhythm we call Baroque. Cows and horses are grouped to combine with the landscape in a great S, and this rhythm is repeated in every detail of roots and rocks. Only the greatest Baroque architects, Bernini and Boromini, had this power of keeping both masses and details moving to the same tune.

Plate 24. From a PORTRAIT OF A BOY (649) ascribed to FRANCESCO ROSSI, painted about 1540.

Plate 25. Mary Gainsborough from THE PAINTER'S DAUGHTERS (1811) by THOMAS GAINSBOROUGH, painted about 1757–58.

There is a superficial likeness between the children, and both painters have enjoyed the delicate contours of their youthful faces. But these resemblances only make more clear a fundamental difference of style. The Italian delineates where Gainsborough suggests. Not to be stiff, this linear style must be done with great mastery, and the eyes of the young Farnese show no real understanding of structure. Mary Gainsborough's eyes are far better drawn. Yet the Italian preserves from a great tradition a more complete sense of plastic unity. He is working within a convention where even a duffer may achieve something if the subject is favourable and he will only keep to the rules.

Plate 26. The Val d'Arno from THE MARTYRDOM OF ST. SEBASTIAN (292) by ANTONIO POLLAIUOLO, painted in 1475. Scale much reduced.

Plate 27. From AUTUMN : THE CHÂTEAU DE STEEN (66) by SIR PETER PAUL R U B E N S, painted about 1635. Scale much reduced.

The background of Rubens's *Autumn* must be one of the greatest of all paintings of a distant landscape ; yet Pollaiuolo's Val d' Arno, a small part of a great figure-piece, withstands the comparison, and we are led to ask why, when landscape had been brought to this pitch of perfection by 1475, it had to wait over a hundred years before being recognised as an independent branch of painting. There is no easy answer. Fifteenth-century painters like Pollaiuolo, Bellini, and Perugino loved the subject and painted it with mastery. Leonardo added science to observation in a way not attempted again until Ruskin's Turner. In part the answer must lie with the Renaissance men of letters who had already evolved the classic theory of aesthetics by which a picture was not serious unless the subject was drawn from sacred or heroic literature. But this theory was even more powerful in the seventeenth century, the first great age of landscape, when Claude and Poussin had to call their pictures by fancy titles in order to give the critics something to write about. We cannot explain this period of landscape by any literary parallel such as can be made to cover the revival of landscape painting in the early nineteenth century. Perhaps the only true explanation is the superficial one : mannerism and eclecticism had so exhausted the figure arts that without the learning of Poussin and the mature endowment of Rubens no further advance in that direction was possible and painters turned to a branch of the art which still allowed some possibility of unforced expression.

These details show an interesting technical point : the difficulty all early landscape painters experienced in passing from the foreground to the background. Pollaiuolo and other early Italian painters evaded this difficulty by placing the scene of action on a plateau so that the middle distance was cut out. Rubens has covered up his failure by brilliance of handling, but if we look carefully we see that the space between the over-life-size partridges and the minute foot-bridge is not realised at all. Claude usually dealt with the problem by a series of *coulisses*. The first painter to whom the middle distance seems to have had no difficulties was Rembrandt, who in his drawings leads the eye smoothly from foreground to background with a few strokes of the pen.

Plate 28. From a LANDSCAPE WITH FIGURES (40) by N I C O L A S POUSSIN, painted about 1648. Scale reduced.

Plate 29. The Death of Jacob from JOSEPH IN EGYPT (1131) by JACOPO P O N T O R M O, painted about 1518.

Two examples of details forming complete compositions in themselves. The Pontormo group must generally pass unnoticed in that weird agglomeration of incidents of which it forms a relatively unimportant part. It is strange that Poussin and Pontormo, who represent to the full two opposed systems of design, classicism and mannerism, should unite so harmoniously ; and no doubt the harmony is partly accidental, due to the looped drapery of the Pontormo echoing the rhythm of Poussin's branches, and the pointing woman who is a principal figure in both scenes. Closer analysis shows how Pontormo has avoided the simple uprights and measured intervals of Poussin, and has achieved a characteristic nervousness, bordering on hysteria. Actually he became an incurable neurasthenic, and kept a diary in which he recorded how many ounces of food he ate at every meal.

Plate 30. King Richard II from THE WILTON DIPTYCH (4451) probably by a

French painter working in England about 1395.

Plate 31. The Vision of St. Francis from SCENES FROM THE LIFE OF ST. FRANCIS OF ASSISI (4757) by SASSETTA, commissioned 1437, finished 1444.

Although separated by fifty years and five hundred miles, these two details unite with perfect harmony. In each a young knight is dedicating himself to some chivalrous ideal. Richard II kneels to receive a Crusader's banner from the Virgin ; Francis dreams of the celestial city. This unity of subject is matched by an equal unity of style, for both artists derive from the gentle, courtly Gothicism of the late fourteenth century, that truly international style which expressed, with half-conscious romanticism, the dying spirit of mediaeval chivalry. The Diptych shows this spirit in its prime. By Sassetta's day it was dead in the North, killed by civil war, social and religious anarchy, and dead in Florence, killed by the fierce intellectual life of the bourgeoisie. Only in Siena, incurably old-fashioned and democratic, was it able to survive and produce in Sassetta its most delicate and imaginative interpreter.

Plate 32. The Feet of Angels from THE BAPTISM (665) by PIERO DELLA FRANCESCA, painted about 1440–45. Scale much reduced.

Plate 33. The Feet of Angels from THE MADONNA OF THE GIRDLE (1155) by MATTEO DI GIOVANNI, painted about 1470. Scale much reduced.

In comparing Piero with his Sienese contemporaries we are inevitably reminded of the contrast between Classical and Gothic architecture, between the columns of a Greek temple and the flying buttresses of a cathedral. In Matteo's *Madonna of the Girdle*, painted about thirty years later than Sassetta's St. Francis series, the character of the individual forms is Gothic no longer, but the movements and silhouettes correspond exactly to those decorative late Gothic traceries which outside of Florence and Rome survived almost to the day when they were transformed into Baroque.

Plate 34. Angels from THE NATIVITY (1034) by SANDRO BOTTICELLI, painted " at the end of the year 1500."

Plate 35. Angels from THE CORONATION OF THE VIRGIN (1897) by LORENZO MONACO, painted about 1415. Scale much reduced.

Analogies between music and painting have led to much loose writing, but everyone can feel some correspondence between visible lines and the lines of a melody ; and these details admit of restatement in terms of music as much, perhaps, as anything in European art. We can follow the main theme rising, falling and being worked out in variations. In the Botticelli the angels on the far side of the circle, moving in the opposite direction, give an extraordinary effect of counterpoint. In the Lorenzo Monaco the undulating chant is slower, but with some steep and surprising cadences. In both the melody is set off by areas of pattern—Lorenzo's diapered floor, Botticelli's olive branches — which are like a *vibrato* accompaniment on the strings. How did this lyrical style come to such perfection in Florence, with its harsh forum life, practical jokes and Cobdenite morality ?

Plate 36. The Virgin's Head from THE MADONNA OF THE GIRDLE (1155) by MATTEO DI GIOVANNI, painted about 1470.

Plate 37. The Virgin's Head from THE VIRGIN AND CHILD WITH ANGELS (275), painted in BOTTICELLI'S WORKSHOP about 1480.

From Vasari's day onwards art-historians have repeated that the serious progressive painting of the fifteenth century was concentrated in Florence, and that Siena was no more than an enchanting backwater. So it is almost a shock to realise that Matteo di Giovanni could conceive a head which from the formal point of view alone is a masterpiece. The outline of the Madonna's face is as simple and momentous as the finest Congo carving ; the concavities of the mask and the elongated eyes also remind us of Negro sculpture. Compared with these large determined arcs, the drawing of the Botticellian Madonna looks very feeble, and we may well ask why for half a century this appealing, but insignificant image should have represented Botticelli in the popular fancy. One answer is that it was almost the first picture of that name to enter the Gallery ; another, more profound, that the public can only swallow a new style with a copious draught of water, and this Madonna provided just the kind of dilution which was necessary when Botticelli's style was still new and difficult. She is the essential pre-Raphaelite Madonna, the origin of those wistful maidens in whom Burne-Jones concealed his natural sensuality.

Plate 38. From THE NATIVITY (1034) by SANDRO BOTTICELLI, painted " at the end of the year 1500."

Plate 39. The Sleeping Apostles from THE AGONY IN THE GARDEN (3476) by EL GRECO, painted about 1600.

Although differing so widely in technique, these two details express the same mood of religious ecstasy in similar language. The figures bend inwards as if under the stress of some magnetic force ; their draperies move in large, rapid, unsensuous arcs, or shoot across the scene in harsh diagonals. Naturally, El Greco can move farther from fact. Mannerism—and he may be regarded by those who enjoy a paradox as the greatest Italian mannerist—allowed a distortion of form never again contemplated until about 1910. But certain details of Botticelli's later work, in particular the Zenobius series, go far towards expressive abstraction. Curiously enough his contemporaries do not seem to have noticed this, and Isabella d'Este's agent in Florence, writing to his mistress in 1502, mentions Botticelli after Perugino and Filippino Lippi as " an excellent painter and one who works willingly and has no hindrances, as the aforesaid." In fact, a good man of business ; and we are reminded that El Greco, too, organised his genius, so that his studio was almost a factory, supplying the whole of Castille with pictures full of genuine mysticism.

Plate 40. Landscape from THE BAPTISM (665) by PIERO DELLA FRANCESCA, painted about 1440–45.

Plate 41. Landscape from THE AGONY IN THE GARDEN (726) by GIOVANNI BELLINI, painted about 1460.

Bellini was the greatest landscape painter of the fifteenth century. Perugino and Pollaiuolo, both of whom were masters of their respective countrysides, Umbria and the Val d'Arno, lacked his variety. He knew how nature appeared at every hour of the day and season of the year ; and was especially fond of the moment of sunset when walled towns and castles on hill-tops catch a light which has already left the plain. It is a moment of great beauty, still to be enjoyed by those who visit Soave, Marostica and others of the few remaining walled towns of the Veneto, and Bellini has used it, without the least exaggeration, to heighten the mood of his most solemn subjects, the Crucifixion or the Agony in the Garden. In this detail the thorny tree, the tortured, winding road and the eventual illumination of the town, seem to symbolise the subject of the picture. But pictorially the landscape needs the sweep of the whole composition and the accents of the figures to give it full value. The background of *The Madonna of the Meadow* (Plate 23) is one of the very few landscapes of the period which do not suffer from isolation.

The landscapes of Piero della Francesca illustrate this fact. Seen in relation to his figures, they are of great importance ; isolated they are almost meaningless. Their value lies in the way they sustain the tone of the picture, that still, silvery atmosphere in which Piero's placid divinities perform their noble actions. This detail from *The Baptism* is of great interest, however, as it shows that the calculating Piero was capable of an apparent freedom which recalls the ink-paintings of the Southern Sung School, or the work of the drunken Wu-Wei. But unlike the Chinese he is without calligraphic flourish, and for this reason the very blottiness of his touch is curiously personal and revealing.

Plate 42. From TENIERS' CHÂTEAU AT PERCK (817) by DAVID TENIERS the Younger, painted 1670–80. Scale reduced.

Teniers is an underrated landscape painter, because his figures, though often beautifully painted in themselves, are never properly related to the background and distract the eye. When they are inconspicuous, as in the *Brickworks* at Dulwich, or when by photography we are able to see a piece of landscape in isolation, we realise that he painted nature in rather the same spirit as Sisley in 1873. He saw the poetry of a prosaic scene and expressed it with a graceful, sensitive

touch. No wonder he was a favourite painter of the English country gentleman, for his backgrounds show that half-conscious understanding of countryside beauty which one finds, so differently expressed, in the letters of Cowper, Cobbett and Edward Fitzgerald.

Plate 43. A Nurseryman pruning Trees from THE AVENUE AT MIDDELHARNIS (930) by MEINDERT HOBBEMA, painted in 1689.

Although this comes from one of the most familiar pictures in the gallery, some people may fail to recognise it at the first glance, since, in looking at the picture as a whole, the eye cannot escape shooting down the central perspective. The idea of making a miniature row of young trees to accompany and, perhaps, later to supplant the main avenue is beyond Hobbema's usual powers of invention. Indeed the whole picture is so far outside his limited range that eminent Dutch critics have doubted its authenticity, and ascribed it, to my mind quite unconvincingly, to a pasticheur named van Kessell.

Plate 44. Still Life from THE AMBASSADORS (1314) by HANS HOLBEIN the Younger, painted in 1533. Scale much reduced.

Plate 45. Still Life from CHRIST IN THE HOUSE OF MARTHA (1375) by VELASQUEZ, painted about 1622.

These two details show two distinct ways in which still life can be made a subject for painting. It may provide the painter with a sort of intellectual game, allied to geometry or counterpoint, in which the winner is he who can combine the most ingenious variety of shapes in two and three dimensions. This is the motive of the earliest piece of postclassical still life known to me, a painting in the Arena Chapel, Padua, presumably by Giotto, which seems to represent a bird-cage. This stage of still life found its fullest expression in the marvellous inlaid woodwork done all over Italy during the Renaissance, much of which was designed by great artists like Baldovinetti and even Piero della Francesca. The geometrical basis of such designs was systematised by Piero's pupil, Pacioli, in his *Divina Proportione* : but there was also a literary element. Certain objects were included on account of their symbolical or evocative qualities. Holbein's still life, in spite of its realism, belongs to this tradition. He even uses the favourite properties of *intarsiatori*, a lute, a globe, open books, geometrical instruments ; but the tradition is already waning and the direct impact of design is weakened by over-realistic detail.

With Velasquez another tradition of still life, originated in part by Caravaggio some twenty-five years earlier, is well established. The artist paints inanimate objects primarily because they keep still. Only thus can he give himself up without distraction to rendering in paint the exact shape, substance and texture of what he sees. Of course, the objects themselves may be arranged in such a way as to form an architectural composition, and may be used to reveal almost the whole range of a painter's sensibility ; but the underlying motive is realism. This detail from Velasquez, then, is the ancestor of Chardin, Bonvin, Manet and, from one point of view, Cézanne. Yet Cézanne led to Cubism, and early Cubism is certainly a return to the still life of the *intarsiatori*. How curious that musical instruments, printed pages and all the old paraphernalia should have reappeared, though the Cubists did not bother to paint each letter on a page, as Holbein has done, but very sensibly gummed pieces of newspaper straight on to the canvas.

Plate 46. From MRS. GRAHAM AS A HOUSEMAID (2928) by THOMAS GAINSBOROUGH, painted about 1776. Scale much reduced.

Plate 47. From LES PARAPLUIES (3268) by AUGUSTE RENOIR, painted about 1880. Scale reduced.

The likeness between Gainsborough and Renoir is familiar to all amateurs, and far more telling examples could be found outside the Gallery ; indeed, these details show the essential difference between them. This may be expressed by the story in Smith's *Life of Nollekens* of how Gainsborough, receiving a letter in a beautiful hand, pinned it on his easel as an inspiration ; whereas Renoir was so little dependent on graceful execution that he painted some of his greatest pictures when, crippled with rheumatism, his brush had to be strapped to his hand. He even created some of his admirable sculpture without touching the clay, simply by pointing with a stick. One cannot imagine Gainsborough producing sculpture at all, and without his handling much of his work would melt away. The head of Mrs. Graham is an extreme example of his elegant flourish, and comes near to superficiality. The girl from *Les Parapluies*, though kept down in tone to the level of the whole composition, has an amplitude which implies a fuller grasp of form.

Plate 48. Philip IV from THE SILVER PHILIP (1129) by VELASQUEZ, painted about 1636.

Plate 49. Charles I from CHARLES I ON HORSEBACK (1172) by SIR ANTHONY VAN DYCK, painted about 1636.

By comparing these two heads of kings, painted perhaps in the same year, we can realise the characters of the two great Court limners of the period. No one doubts that Velasquez was the greater artist, but *The Silver Philip*, painted as a display of brilliant handling, does not do justice to his finest qualities. The head of Charles I, on the other hand, shows van Dyck at his best, and at first sight looks solider than its neighbour. This is partly due to photography, which always flatters pictures painted in glazes over a monochrome foundation at the expense of direct painting in colour. A great deal of the modelling in Philip's face is in pure colour and disappears in black and white, and the breadth and subtlety of Velasquez's handling is only visible in the mouth and hair. What survives photography, however, is his detached vision. Philip IV looked like that. Charles I wanted to look like that, and van Dyck has subtly interpreted his sitter's romantic egotism. That is the aim of every fashionable portrait painter; and to-day no one who is devoid of this gift can hope to make more than a bare livelihood out of the art of painting.

Plate 50. Jean de Dinteville, Lord of Polisy, from THE AMBASSADORS (1314) by HANS HOLBEIN the Younger, painted in 1533.

Plate 51. From CHRISTINA OF DENMARK, DUCHESS OF MILAN (2475) by HANS HOLBEIN the Younger, painted in 1538. Scale reduced.

Photographic details may help to redress our scale of values. *The Ambassadors* is a large panel, full of distracting properties, and we fail to realise that the heads are among the masterpieces of Holbein's portraiture. They are also well preserved, whereas poor Christina has suffered considerably. Her cheeks are covered with retouches, and her left eye is almost entirely gone over. This is clear when we compare the photograph of her head with the plate

opposite, but in the original the simplicity and concentration of the whole design is so effective that we are not too critical of such details, and see her as what she once was—the most moving of all Holbein's larger portraits.

Plate 52. From MADAME MOITESSIER, SEATED (4821) by JEAN-AUGUSTE-DOMINIQUE INGRES, begun in 1847, finished in 1856.

Madame Moitessier was a famous beauty. That is an aspect of the subject which it is difficult for us to realise—difficult, but essential, for Ingres felt it acutely and made it the basis of his design. She represents beauty enthroned, like a Phoenician goddess, half Roman, half Oriental, calmly aware of her feminine potency. Contemporary taste seems to find this self-confidence irritating, and the head which Ingres referred to as *terrible et belle*, repulsive. Even her hand which delighted Gautier has been abused for its lack of bony structure. By 1856 Ingres had been acclaimed for forty years as the greatest draughtsman in Europe; none of his contemporaries had been so foolish as to say that his hands were " out of drawing," and we must, I fear, conclude that a sense of plastic coherency is less common now than it was in that derided epoch of taste, the mid-nineteenth century. For whatever we may think of her as a beauty, Madame Moitessier is a masterpiece of formal construction. There is a largeness and continuity in every sequence of form which makes her neighbours look haphazard, and apparent defects of painting spring from deliberate subordination to a central idea.

Plate 53. Head of Susanna Fourment from LE CHAPEAU DE PAILLE (852) by SIR PETER PAUL RUBENS,] painted about 1625-30.

This is a study of the contrast between Susanna Fourment's delicate complexion and her dark eyes ; and to give this contrast its full effect Rubens has painted her under a hat the tone of her eyes, with her face lit by reflected light, so that all dark shadows are eliminated, leaving only the local colours of lips, eyebrows and iris. Illumination by reflected light usually means rather flat painting, but Rubens has been able to keep the modelling alive at every point with a delicacy and transparency which is his secret, and with such apparent ease that we think more of his enchanting sitter than of his superb technical skill.

Plate 54. A Cat from THE GRAHAM CHILDREN (4756) by WILLIAM HOGARTH, painted in 1742.

Plate 55. A Dog from THE DEATH OF PROCRIS (698) by PIERO DI COSIMO, painted about 1500.

Hogarth enjoyed painting this cat so much that the Graham children look hollow and lifeless beside her. She is the embodiment of cockney vitality, alert and adventurous— a sort of Nell Gwynn among cats. Her vulgarity would hardly be noticeable, were she not confronted by the noble silhouette of Piero's hound who regards her with the gravity of an antique philosopher. Paul Bourget, when asked what Walter Pater looked like, replied " Il ressemblait à un amant de Circe transformé en dogue."

Plate 56. Cupid from MERCURY INSTRUCTING CUPID BEFORE VENUS (10) by CORREGGIO, painted about 1530.

Plate 57. Cupid from THE ROKEBY VENUS (2057) by VELASQUEZ, painted about 1650–55. Scale much reduced.

Similarity of subject makes clear the great difference in handling. Correggio, in spite of his love of softness, begins from definition by drawing. The forms are modelled and then glazed. Velasquez has also used glazes in the flesh parts ; but his Cupid's head, hair and wings are painted with a directness which no sixteenth-century painter, except perhaps Tintoretto, would have considered decent ; and the Cupid's left leg would have shocked Correggio, though it may be compared to the left hand of Tintoretto's princess on Plate 66.

Plate 58. Hands from HELENA FOURMENT (?) by SIR PETER PAUL RUBENS, painted about 1635. (Lent by Mr. C. S. Gulbenkian.)

Plate 59. Hands from CHRISTINA OF DENMARK, DUCHESS OF MILAN (2475) by HANS HOLBEIN, painted in 1538.

These hands illustrate the Renaissance and Baroque principles of composition. Behind Holbein's conception is an enclosed geometrical form like a pyramid. Rubens is thinking of a landscape with undulating hills and waterfalls.

Plate 60. Venus from MERCURY INSTRUCTING CUPID BEFORE VENUS (10) by CORREGGIO, painted about 1530. Scale reduced.

How perfectly *dix-huitième* Correggio was ! This detail should have been placed opposite a Nattier, if there had been a suitable one in the Gallery. There is something disconcerting about an artist who belongs so completely to an epoch other than his own. Any work of art must vibrate in the memory, but the resonances of a Correggio are so insistent and unexpected that our true sense of values is distracted. Before we have had time to look at his pictures for their own sakes we have begun mentally to relate them to the stylistic development of the seventeenth and eighteenth centuries. If it could be established that Correggio, like "Ercole Grandi," was the invention of some early art-historian, and that all his pictures were painted at a later date, how should we value him? I think we should say that he was the greatest painter of the eighteenth century, with a wider range than Watteau, a finer sense of beauty than Boucher, and a solider core than Fragonard.

Plate 61. Alexander from THE FAMILY OF DARIUS BEFORE ALEXANDER (294) by PAOLO VERONESE, painted about 1570.

It is typical of Veronese's lack of interest in drama (see note to Plate 18) that he should have made no attempt to recreate the historical Alexander—still less, it will be remembered, the family of Darius. His subject is a young Venetian model, painted with a breadth and directness which looks the more striking by contrast with the feminine subtleties of Correggio. A hundred years earlier Mantegna would have ransacked his friends' collections for coins, gems, and reliefs which might give him a correct idea of Alexander's appearance. This archaeological enthusiasm died out of painting early in the sixteenth century, but still survived in architecture, thanks to the authority of Vitruvius; and the backgrounds of Veronese's pictures contain examples of high Renaissance architecture freer and more imaginative than those actually constructed.

Plate 62. From THE DEATH OF ST. PETER MARTYR (41) by CARIANI, painted about 1510–15. Scale reduced.

Plate 63. From ST. GEORGE AND THE DRAGON (16) by JACOPO TINTORETTO, painted about 1570. Scale reduced.

It is a proof of the rapid growth of Venetian romanticism under Giorgione's influence that a detail from Cariani goes well enough opposite Tintoretto's St. George. A detail from Bellini's picture of the same subject which hangs on the same wall in the Gallery would look quite set and *quattrocento*, although it cannot have been painted more than ten years earlier. So strong was the influence of this romantic mood in Venice that, like Raphael's classicism in Rome, it was the subject of a series of revivals throughout the sixteenth century, thus producing the many hundreds of pictures formerly labelled "Giorgione," under which name, in fact, the picture under discussion passed into the Gallery in 1831. There is nothing in Italian art more romantic than Tintoretto's St. George. Even the knights and Moroccans of Delacroix look relatively prosaic beside him, because Delacroix never allowed himself such extravagant effects of illumination. We have to look for parallels in non-Mediterranean painting—in Altdorfer's *Battle of Alexander* or in Turner's *Ulysses deriding Polyphemus*.

Plate 64. From BACCHUS AND ARIADNE (35) by TITIAN, painted about 1520. Scale much reduced.

The baby satyr is one of the most charming inhabitants of the National Gallery; but how much of him is original? Until the discoloured varnish has been removed it is impossible to know, and personally I do not think the knowledge worth the appalling risks involved. We can guess by analogy with Titian's other Bacchanals that the *Bacchus and Ariadne* must be covered with minor damages, but these are well concealed by ancient retouchings and a dark, golden varnish; although the general tone of the picture must be very different from what it was in Titian's lifetime, it has a unity and richness which cleaning would almost certainly destroy.

Plate 65. A Lion and a Bear from THE VIRGIN AND CHILD WITH ST. JEROME AND ST. DOMINIC (293) by FILIPPINO L I P P I, painted about 1480.

Even those who know the Gallery well may not have recognised the source of this amusing detail, which reminds us more of Piero di Cosimo than Filippino. By selecting such passages as these the camera can show us how much fantasy and invention the Renaissance artists were forced, by the serious nature of their commissions, to squeeze into their backgrounds, or to express in ephemeral decorations, pageants and masquerades now completely lost to us.

Plate 66. The Princess from ST. GEORGE AND THE DRAGON (16) by JACOPO T I N T O R E T T O, painted about 1560 (?). Scale much reduced.

Plate 67. Bacchus from BACCHUS AND ARIADNE (35) by T I T I A N, painted about 1520. Scale much reduced.

No opening in the book is less in need of comment ; or rather any useful comment would have to fill a volume, for it would turn into an answer to the question how artists came to give unity, movement and colour to their subjects by the convention of flying draperies. In art we are so used to voluminous draperies, fluttering in a wind which often fails to disturb the surrounding foliage, that we forget how uncommonly this happens in life. It is, of course, a convention of Greek art, found as early as the Mausoleum and the Nereid monument, but owing its diffusion to the innumerable sarcophagi which derived in style from the Pergamene school. These sarcophagi were the chief sources of classical art known to the Middle Ages and the early Renaissance ; but in addition fluttering draperies must have been

common in the illustrations to classical manuscripts, and thence they are transposed into the Utrecht psalter and its numerous derivatives ; thus they influenced such pieces of pure Romanesque sculpture as the prophets of Moissac, which were generally taken from manuscript illustrations. This takes us a long way from Bacchus, but he is not so far from the Hellenistic sarcophagi, and we can understand why this convention had such authority in the Renaissance. What a magnificent pictorial convention it was, allowing a painter to unite two groups with a flood of moving colour and to put a great splash of white or crimson against a blue sky. He could frame a head, and hide an awkward plane, and keep a dull passage alive : in fact, flowing drapery was almost as useful to the Italian of the sixteenth and seventeenth centuries as cloud to the Chinese landscape painter of the Sung and Yuan dynasties. No wonder this invaluable means became an end in itself, so that in Bernini and the Baroque painters drapery is all. In this detail and elsewhere Tintoretto shows us how far the convention can be ridden without its taking the bit between its teeth. He always subordinates drapery to the design as a whole, and the vitality of his handling prevents it from ever having the mere windiness of Pozzo or Pietro da Cortona.

Plate 68. The Young Bronzino from JOSEPH IN EGYPT (1131) by JACOPO P O N T O R M O, painted about 1518.

Plate 69. The Children of Andrea Vendramin from THE VENDRAMIN FAMILY (4452) by T I T I A N, painted about 1545. Scale much reduced.

These two sets of children show the nervous, sentimental elaboration of Florentine painting in its decline and the robust materialism of Venetian painting at its zenith. Only in the Titian the boy with the dog is slightly romanticised, and perhaps was worked on by van Dyck, to whom the picture once belonged. In his description of the Pontormo, Vasari tells us that the little boy on the steps is the young Bronzino ; and as Vasari was a great admirer of the picture and knew Bronzino well personally, this is certainly correct. He entered Pontormo's studio at an early age, and in the picture can hardly be more than fifteen years old. This would mean that Pontormo was under twenty-four when he painted it, but he has already evolved his curious, intricate, personal style. He was, in fact, one of the most precocious of Italian painters, with the usual result that his later work suffers from a kind of fastidious exhaustion.

Plate 70. Landscape from "NOLI ME TANGERE" (270) by TITIAN (?) painted about 1510–15. Scale reduced.

Plate 71. Landscape from MADONNA AND CHILD WITH ST. JOHN AND ST. CATHERINE (635) by TITIAN (?) painted about 1530 (?).

The group of buildings in Plate 70 should be famous in the history of landscape painting for it occurs, in almost identical form, in Giorgione's *Venus* at Dresden, and reversed in Titian's *Sacred and Profane Love.* Of these versions, that in the background of our "*Noli me Tangere*" is by far the most delicately painted, and I am inclined to accept the hypothesis recently put forward that it and other parts of the picture are from the hand of Giorgione. Paradoxically enough, the version in the Dresden *Venus* seems to be by Titian who, Michiel tells us, finished the picture. This is an occasion when a question of connoisseurship is worth considering ; for the inventor of this lovely motive must be reckoned one of the great prophets of landscape painting. Who else,

besides Rembrandt, has achieved this combination of architectural grandeur and atmosphere, mystery and peace ?

The detail on the opposite page looks coarse and clumsy by comparison. From the photograph we may even doubt if it is by Titian, but the original shows an observation of nature expressed with great force of colour which is convincing.

Plate 72. From THE ADORATION OF THE MAGI (1033) by SANDRO BOTTICELLI, painted about 1475. Scale reduced.

Plate 73. From ESTHER BEFORE AHASUERUS (1430) by DOMENICO BECCAFUMI, painted about 1540–45. Scale much reduced.

The round arches and emphatic verticals in the Beccafumi are echoed in the Botticelli ; even the sweeping dresses of Esther's attendants find a much amplified counterpart in Botticelli's peacock. Beccafumi is an underrated artist. With his lively handling and quick eye for an amusing silhouette he is the ancestor of Guardi, Callot, and Sickert, and shares their love of artificial light. Even his big machines, painted under the influence of Roman mannerism, are redeemed by brilliant effects of lighting, flames, night scenes, or sunshine streaming into a dark place.

Plate 74. From THE NATIVITY (1034) by SANDRO BOTTICELLI, painted at the end of 1500.

Plate 75. From THE BATTLE OF CENTAURS AND LAPITHS (4890) by PIERO DI COSIMO, painted about 1500. Scale much reduced.

Perhaps sacred and profane love. Botticelli has expressed the disembodied joy of certain passages in the *Paradiso*, but as a rule the sacred love of the mystics is far more sensuous. Language, even the language of Oriental eroticism, can be interpreted symbolically, but shapes declare themselves without equivocation. So in this phase of Puritanism, Botticelli, the most delicate master of sensuous beauty, must hide the human body in voluminous, unrevealing draperies. Piero di Cosimo's Centaur and Centauress are extraordinarily touching. To their human tenderness is added a dumb animal pathos of which he is the unique interpreter. This group is so absorbing as poetry that we do not at once realise the skill with which Piero di Cosimo has solved an unusual problem : how to make a good composition out of two recumbent centaurs. Their inverted heads and the elaborate arabesque of their arms show a mastery of design which he never surpassed.

Plate 76. An Archer from THE MARTYRDOM OF ST. SEBASTIAN (292) by ANTONIO POLLAIUOLO, painted in 1475.

Plate 77. Envy from VENUS, CUPID, FOLLY AND TIME (651) by ANGELO BRONZINO, painted about 1546.

This magnificent opening shows the continuity of the Florentine tradition. The two pictures are separated by almost seventy years, yet both painters are interested in the same forms, and depict them with the same balance of line and modelling. Only in Envy's expression do we feel a shade of exaggeration, deriving no doubt from Leonardo's *Battle of Anghiari*, which reminds us that Bronzino lived in the age of mannerism.

Plate 78. Mars from MARS AND VENUS (915) by SANDRO BOTTICELLI, painted about 1485.

Even in Botticelli's day a fine fore-shortening was considered a proof of capacity. But he sets about his problems in a spirit very different from that of Mantegna or of those German artists whom Dürer has shown us drawing the foreshortened figure through a squared projector. His aim is not accuracy but expressiveness. A drawing-master might make some corrections in Mars's head, but these would certainly destroy the movement of the planes and the feeling of utter relaxation which is its chief beauty.

Plate 79. Masks from VENUS, CUPID, FOLLY AND TIME (651) by ANGELO BRONZINO, painted about 1546.

Classical masks play an important part in the late Renaissance, since they were one of the few ways in which the grotesque, the unreal, the gargoyle element in art could be introduced with propriety. Even Michelangelo put them into the Medici Chapel, and Bronzino may have had in mind the noble mask which lies beside the figure of Night when he designed the masks in this detail. It is the sort of homage which the Florentine academics would have been glad to pay to their divinity. Actually Bronzino's masks have a literary significance, for they lie at the feet of Fraud and Folly, and are part of the allegory of passion which is the real subject of the picture.

Plate 80. From THE MADONNA AND CHILD (296) by ANDREA DEL VERROCCHIO, painted about 1470. Scale reduced.

Plate 81. From THE MADONNA AND CHILD, ST. JOHN AND ANGELS (809) by MICHELANGELO, painted about 1494.

The authenticity of the Michelangelo has often been questioned, and the best critical opinion is still against it, but a comparison of these two details speaks strongly in its favour. In general movement they are remarkably alike. They clearly belong to the same tradition, and no one seeing them together could maintain, as has been done, that the Michelangelo is by a late sixteenth-century mannerist. On the other hand they are strikingly different, and only a great artist could make Verrocchio look so feeble and conventional. In spite of a certain youthful clumsiness, Michelangelo's Madonna has true, unmistakable force and nobility, perceptible in every touch. This detail shows clearly the strokes of the brush like strokes of the chisel on a block of marble which will remind every amateur of Michelangelo's early pen drawings.

Plate 82. The Virgin from THE ANSIDEI MADONNA (1171) by RAPHAEL, painted in 1506.

Raphael sails very near the wind. Cold, insipid, complacent, academic—all these words are on the tips of our tongues, as they are when we read certain passages of Racine, and with as little justification. What saves him? First of all his supreme skill, of which this head shows one aspect, the economy with which he could achieve an unsurpassed degree of plastic fullness. And then there is in Raphael, as in Racine and Mozart, an inner rhythm which is perceptible in every touch, and allows great precision without loss of grace or vitality. From another hand the drawing of the Virgin's eyes would have been schematic; and the parallel shading round her cheek would have been as lifeless as a line engraving. With Raphael all the weapons of academic technique become as sensitive and springy as a rapier.

Plate 83. From THE VIRGIN OF THE ROCKS (1093) by LEONARDO DA VINCI and an assistant, painted about 1506.

There is no longer any doubt that our *Virgin of the Rocks* is a second version of the subject undertaken by Leonardo some twenty years after the picture in the Louvre. Exactly why he was commissioned to paint this later version is unknown, but a most probable reason is that the original had been sent to France at the order of Louis XII, and Leonardo was asked to make a replica for the Congregatione della Carità to which the original had belonged. It is uncertain how much of this replica he executed with his own hand, and this head of the Virgin is the most difficult part of the problem. It is too heavy and lifeless for Leonardo and the actual type is un-Leonardesque; yet it seems to be painted in exactly the same technique as the angel's head in the same picture; and that is so perfect that surely Leonardo must have had a hand in it. Both show curious marks of palm and thumb (they are visible in this detail) made when the paint was wet, and no doubt covered by glazes long since removed. This perhaps is a clue to the problem. A pupil did the main work of drawing and modelling, and before his paint was dry Leonardo put in the finishing touches. Most of these have been removed from the Virgin's face but remain in the angel's, where perhaps they were always more numerous.

Plate 84. From THE MADONNA AND CHILD (566) by DUCCIO, painted about 1290.

Plate 85. From THE MADONNA AND CHILD (3046) by MASACCIO, painted in 1426. Scale much reduced.

Between these two Madonnas there lies the emergence of that new scheme of human values which was one of the great conquests of Renaissance art. The Duccio is not lacking in tenderness, but this only makes itself felt to one whose eye is accustomed to his style. He speaks to us in an ancient, elegant, formal language, perfected two hundred years earlier in Constantinople, xxvi

after centuries of attrition. Even Masaccio's
Madonna shows some memory of this style
in the large rhythms of the composition ; but
essentially she is a new creation, born of a
direct and serious contemplation of nature.
Never before and seldom again has a painter
had the courage to make his Madonna a
plain, natural woman who does not derive
her authority from conventional beauty, but
from the moral grandeur latent in her expression. Compared with her, the Madonnas of
Giotto and Michelangelo are too imperious,
those of Botticelli and Fra Filippo too
pathetic : only Bellini, in the Brera *Pietà*,
has created a similar type of common
humanity raised to the divine.

Plate 86. The Angel Gabriel from THE
ANNUNCIATION (666) by FRA FILIPPO
LIPPI, painted about 1445–50. Scale
much reduced.

Plate 87. An Angel from THE MADONNA
AND CHILD (3046) by MASACCIO,
painted in 1426. Scale reduced.

Fra Filippo's angel expresses that same
Florentine feeling for graceful movement
which we find in Lorenzo Monaco and
Botticelli (Plates 34 and 35). It stands in
time midway between them. We see that
this linear tradition in Florentine art was
unbroken, and expressed a more continuous
need than the tradition of scientific naturalism, of which Masaccio's angel is a small but
sturdy representative. Up to a point it is
true to say that this linear style was popular
and aristocratic, whereas the solid, scientific
style of Masaccio was only appreciated by
the humanists and intellectual bourgeoisie.
Yet Fra Filippo was a favourite painter of the
Medici, and *The Annunciation* was almost
certainly painted for Cosimo Pater Patriae.

Plate 88. An Angel from THE VIRGIN
AND CHILD (296) by ANDREA DEL
VERROCCHIO, painted about 1470.

Plate 89. Two Angels from THE
MADONNA OF THE GIRDLE (1155)
by MATTEO DI GIOVANNI,
painted about 1470.

As a comparison between Sienese and
Florentine painting this is unfair on Florence,
because Matteo's picture is one of the masterpieces of its school, which Verrocchio's is
not. In fact, it is little more than a piece of
high-class craftsmanship, the kind of picture
you bought at a goldsmith's shop, where you
might also buy the original of the pretty
brooch worn by the Angel. However, it
serves to show the chief aims of Florentine
drawing : to make the human form look
solid. The Sienese thought of drawing as
involving balance of line and pattern. In
the detail from Matteo di Giovanni, wings,
draperies and the musical instrument are
an accompaniment to the angels' heads,
whereas in the Verrocchio they are only a
distraction.

Plate 90. St. Francis gives his Cloak to
a poor Gentleman, from SCENES FROM
THE LIFE OF ST. FRANCIS OF ASSISI
(4757) by SASSETTA, commissioned
1437, finished 1444.

Plate 91. From THE BAPTISM (665) by
PIERO DELLA FRANCESCA,
painted about 1440–45. Scale reduced.

Most of the comparisons in this book
bridge wide intervals of time and space ;
this one is the reverse. Piero's *Baptism* and
Sassetta's *Scenes from the Life of St. Francis
of Assisi* were painted for the small town of
Borgo san Sepolcro in the same years, and
both artists were influenced by the same
masters, Masolino and, in particular,
Domenico Veneziano. From the latter they
derived a pale, luminous atmosphere which
Sassetta soon abandoned, but which Piero
made one of the bases of his style.

Though temporarily united by this joy in silvery tone, they are essentially different. Sassetta is still Gothic. His road shoots up at an impossible angle, and all his forms harmonise with this sharp Gothic movement. The curve of Piero's river bank is slow and classical. All his forms have the measured deliberation of antique architecture, and the man taking off his shirt, which Vasari praised for its naturalism, might have come from the Acropolis.

Plate 92. From THE VIRGIN AND CHILD WITH ST. JOHN AND ANGELS (809) by MICHELANGELO, painted about 1494 (?).

Plate 93. From THE CIRCUMCISION (1128) by SIGNORELLI, painted about 1492–94 (?).

Signorelli was one of the most consistently serious of all great artists. He never allowed himself any of the humour or fantasy which we find in almost all the painters of the Renaissance, and even his *Triumph of Pan* in the Berlin Gallery is conceived in terms of great solemnity. This seriousness, no less than his interest in the nude, is his link with Michelangelo. If, as I believe, our *Virgin and Child* is by the young Michelangelo, it probably dates from before his visit to Orvieto in 1496; yet the affinity with Signorelli is already obvious. In a note to Plates 80 and 81 I have given some reasons why the old attribution of our picture to Michelangelo cannot be dismissed without consideration. In this detail it is worth noticing how closely these two youths resemble, in character and morphology, the figure carved by Michelangelo for the Ark of St. Dominic, Bologna, in 1494; and in particular the St. Proculus which, I would suggest, is a self-portrait of Michelangelo himself as a young man.

Plate 94. St. John from THE ENTOMBMENT (790) by MICHELANGELO, painted about 1505 (?). Scale reduced.

Plate 95. A Group of Women from THE RAISING OF LAZARUS (1) by SEBASTIANO DEL PIOMBO, painted in 1517–19. Scale much reduced.

The Grand Manner, that painful obsession of European art, is a personal endowment. It is like a noble gesture which cannot be imitated without becoming empty and theatrical. In no one has this endowment been so strong as in Michelangelo who, from his earliest youth, could not make a mark which was devoid of grandeur; with the result that for centuries ambitious artists were led to their ruin. Sebastiano del Piombo was the first of the long line which culminated in Benjamin Robert Haydon: not that the Grand Manner drove Sebastiano to suicide, only it left him so exhausted that after receiving a pension from the Pope he never painted again and lived solely for gossip and the pleasures of the table. His efforts to assume the Grand Manner were remarkably successful, for he was close to the source of that dangerous illumination. It was easier for him to glow with reflected glory when Michelangelo stood beside him, and, as we are told, even provided drawings for *The Raising of Lazarus*. We can believe that the group in this detail, which in sentiment and to some extent in form anticipates that unforgettable group of women in the Capella Paolina fresco of *St. Peter's Crucifixion*, derives from a sketch by Michelangelo who often foreshadowed in his studies motives which were only brought to mature expression many years later.

Plate 96. From PIETÀ (3912) by GIOVANNI BELLINI, painted about 1475. Scale reduced.

Often in his treatment of solemn themes Bellini indulges in conscious archaism, and this is particularly true of the period round about 1475 when his Madonnas show the influence of Byzantine painting. The Mond *Pietà* belongs to these years, and in this detail the angel's head is deliberately archaic. This simplified oval has the added value that it does not distract from the complex plastic sequences of the head of Christ.

Plate 97. The Angel's Head from THE VIRGIN OF THE ROCKS (1093) by LEONARDO DA VINCI and an assistant, painted about 1506.

This is the one part of our *Virgin of the Rocks* where the evidence of Leonardo's hand seems undeniable, not only in the full, simple modelling, but in the drawing of the hair. The curls round the shoulder have exactly the same movement as Leonardo's drawings of swirling water. Beautiful as it is, this angel lacks the enchantment of the lighter, more Gothic angel in the Paris version. It embodies the result of Leonardo's later researches in which ideal beauty and classic regularity of chiaroscuro were combined, with a certain loss in freshness, but with an expressive power which almost hypnotized his contemporaries.

Plate 98. The Sleeping Apostles from THE AGONY IN THE GARDEN (1417) by ANDREA MANTEGNA, painted about 1460. Scale reduced.

Plate 99. The Sleeping Apostles from THE AGONY IN THE GARDEN (726) by GIOVANNI BELLINI, painted about 1460. Scale reduced.

It is a piece of wonderful good fortune that two great pictures of the same subject, probably painted at the same time by men who were intimately related to one another, should hang on the same wall in the National Gallery ; and in comparing them generations of amateurs must have learnt one of their first and finest lessons in the appreciation of Italian art. The comparison provided by these two details of the Sleeping Apostles is unfair on Bellini. His drawing looks cramped and immature beside the grasp and grandeur of Mantegna. We can understand why he always spoke of his brother-in-law with such deep respect and, even in old age, wrote to Isabella d'Este that he did not feel worthy to paint in a room already decorated by Mantegna. (However, this may only have been an excuse to avoid working for a troublesome patron.) Yet even in this detail we are aware of Bellini's unrivalled feeling for light, and his Apostles have a human pathos which makes Mantegna seem a little too intellectual. A wise critic in 1460, comparing the work of these two youngish artists, might have admitted Mantegna's greater mastery but seen in Bellini a passionate love of nature which promised a fuller development. And in fact Mantegna remained set in his classic mould, while Bellini revealed, till past his eightieth year, new depths of poetry and humanity.

Plate 100. The Crucifixion from THE VISION OF ST. EUSTACE (1436) by PISANELLO, painted before 1438. Scale enlarged to twice actual size.

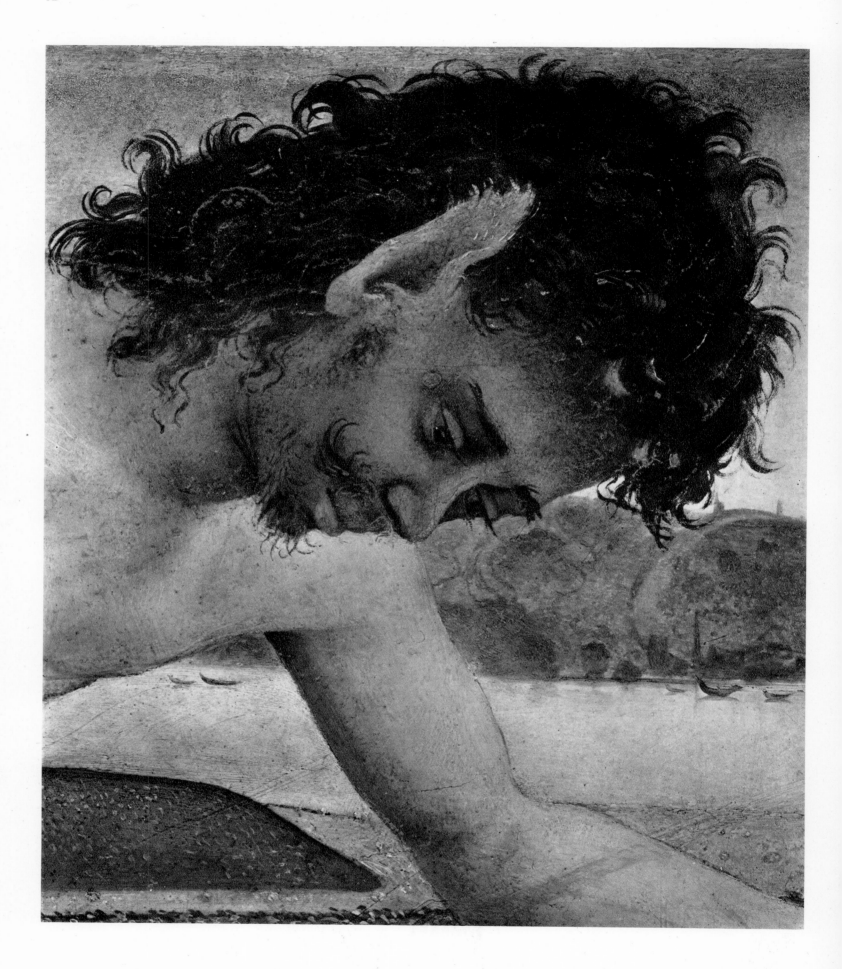

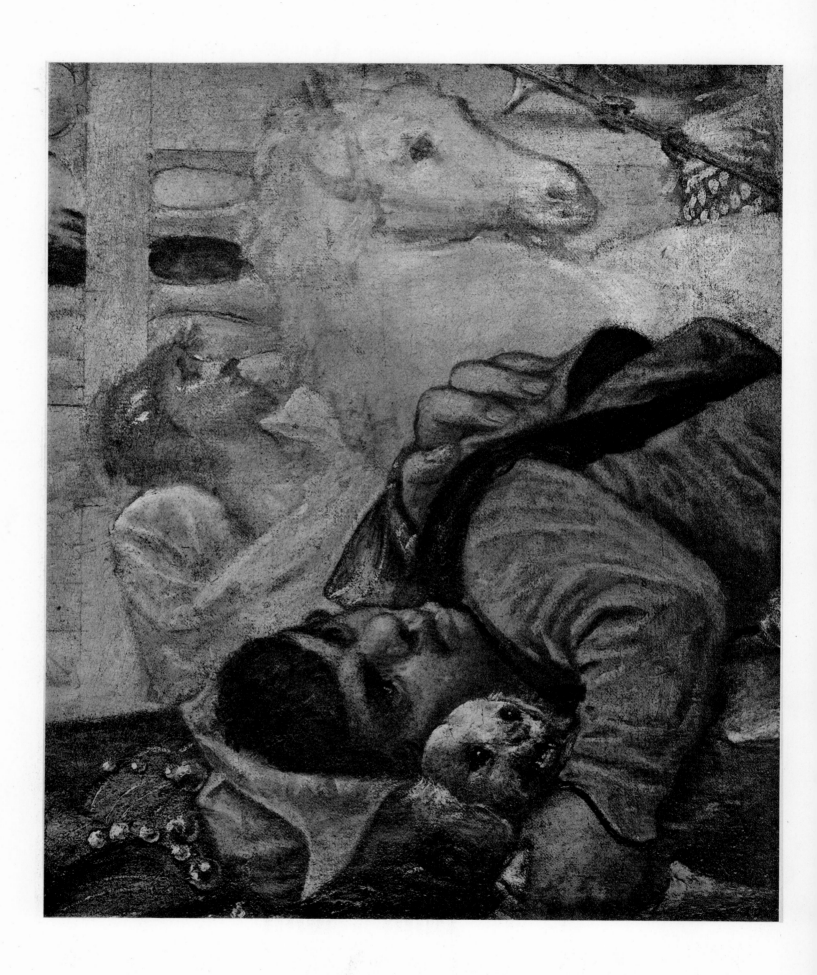

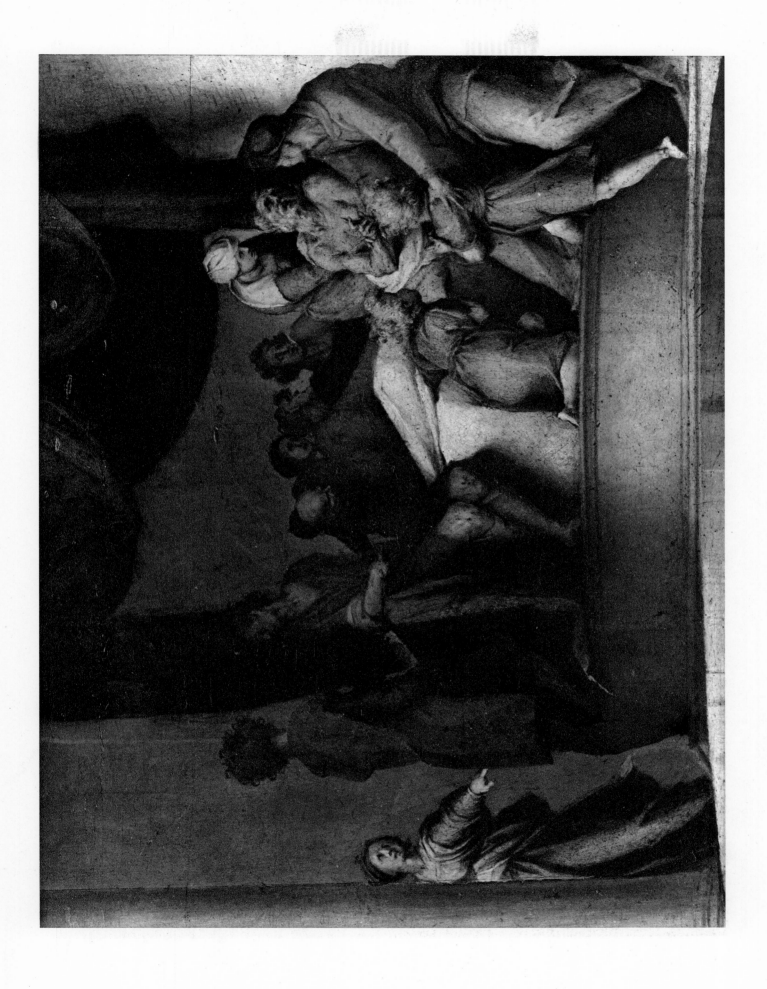

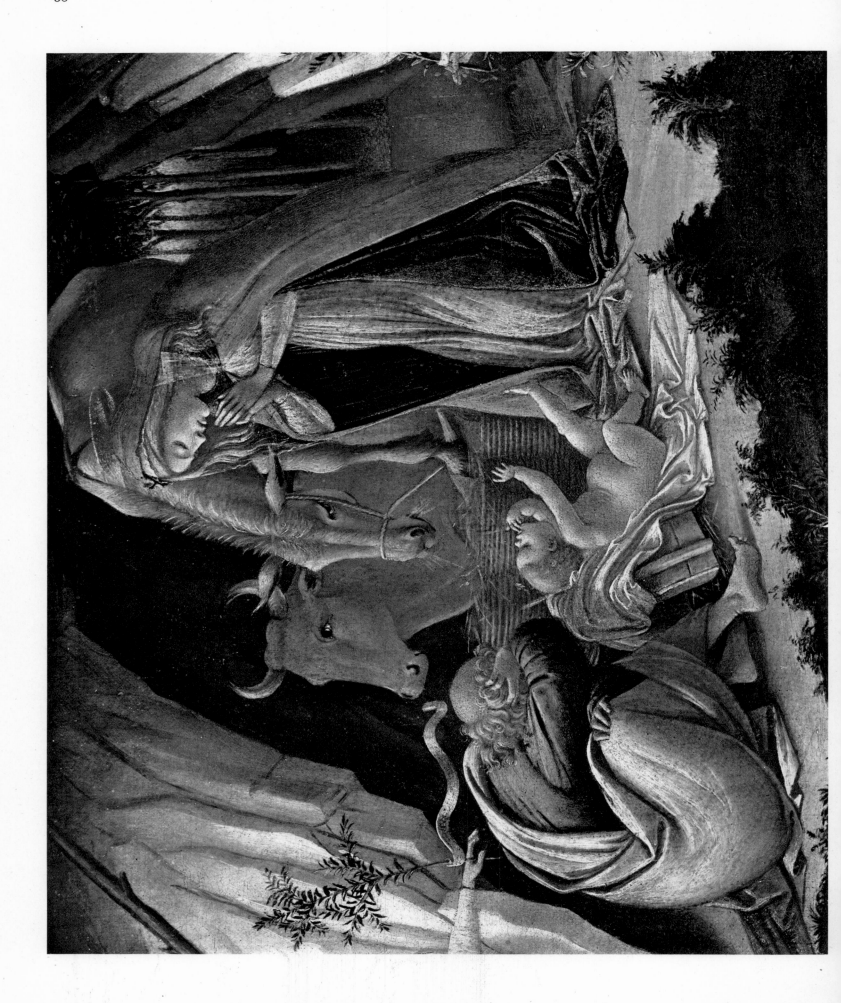

41

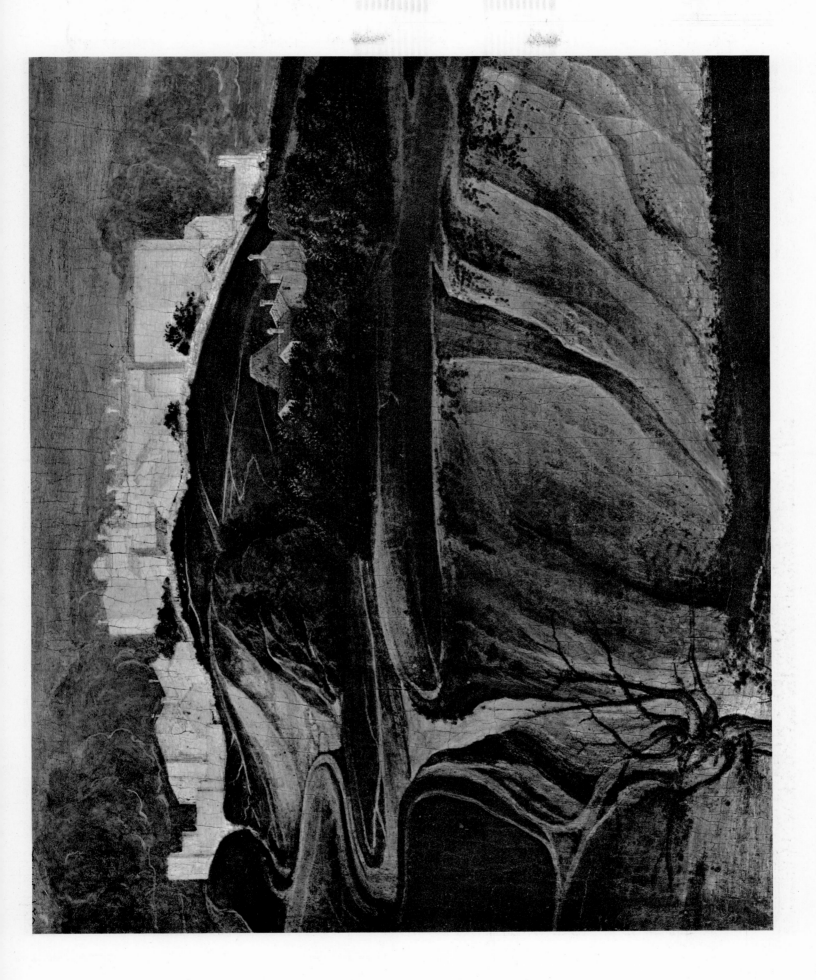

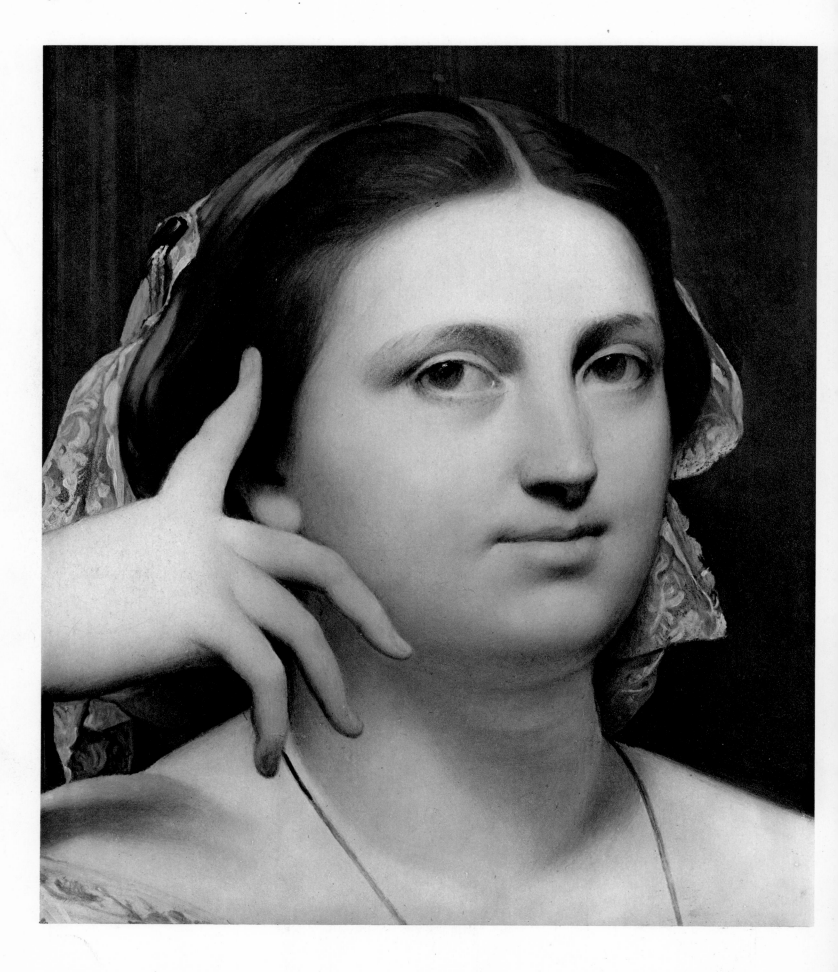

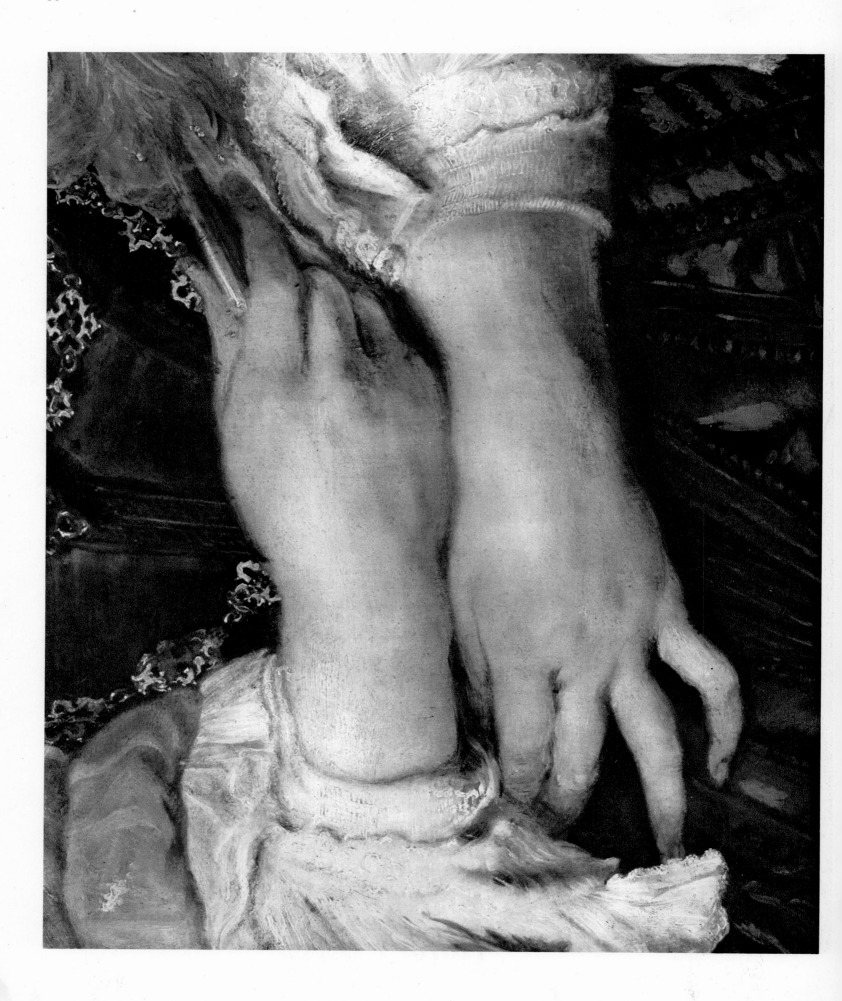

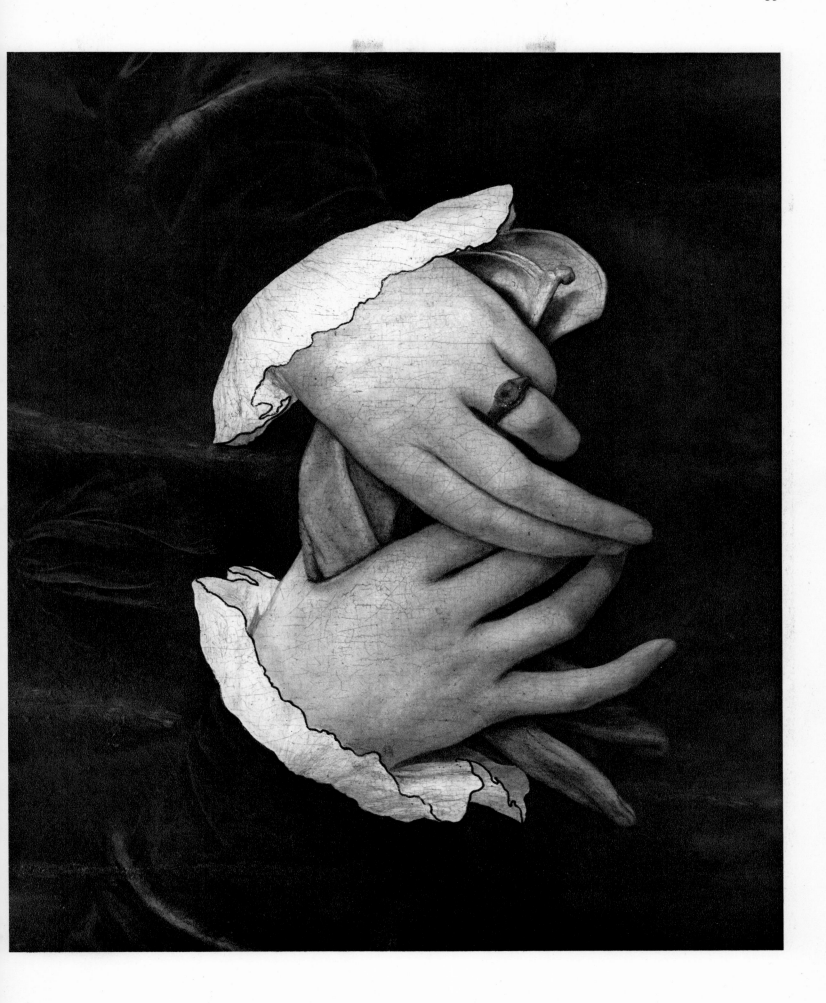

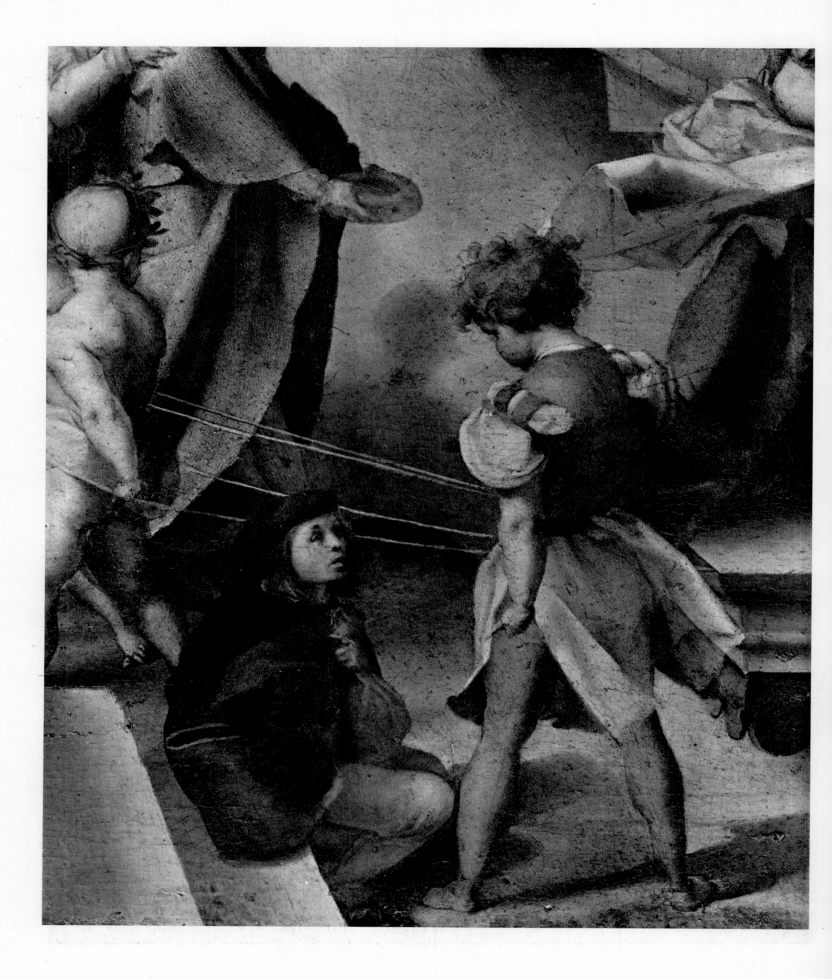

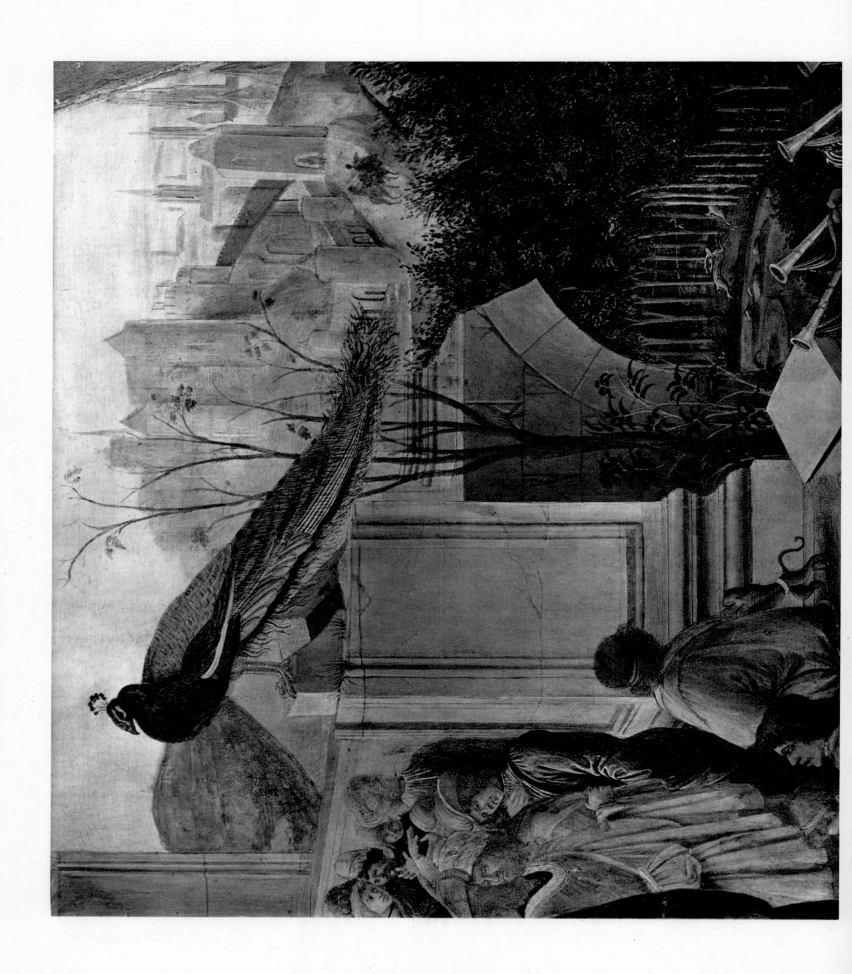

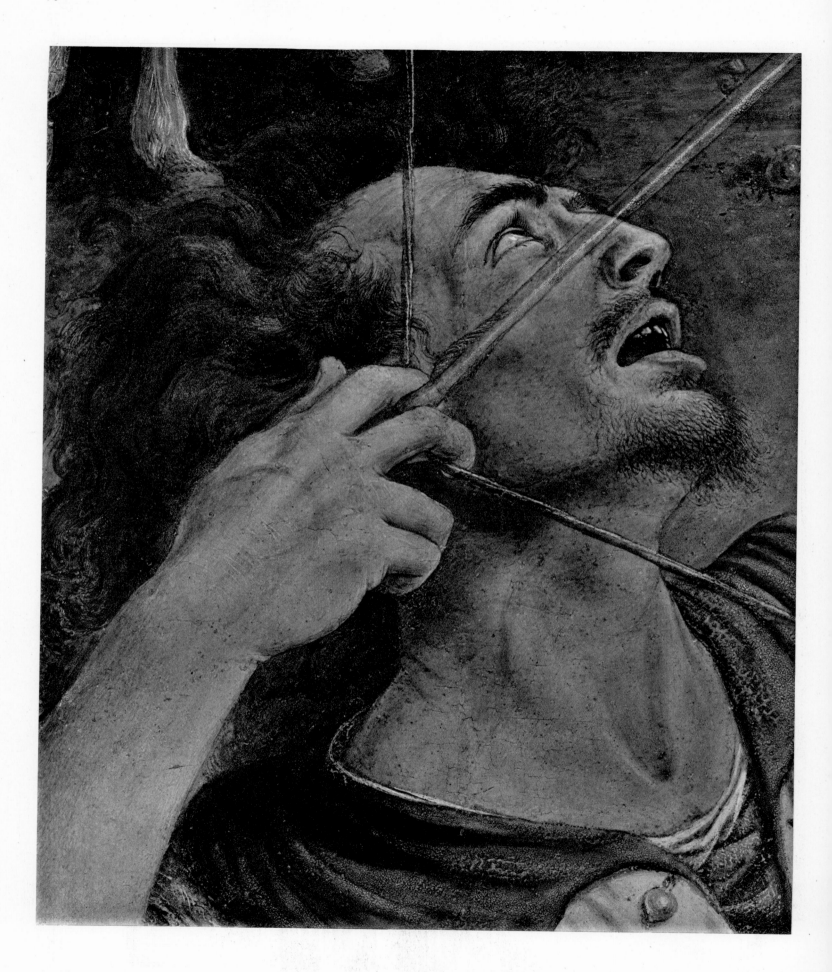

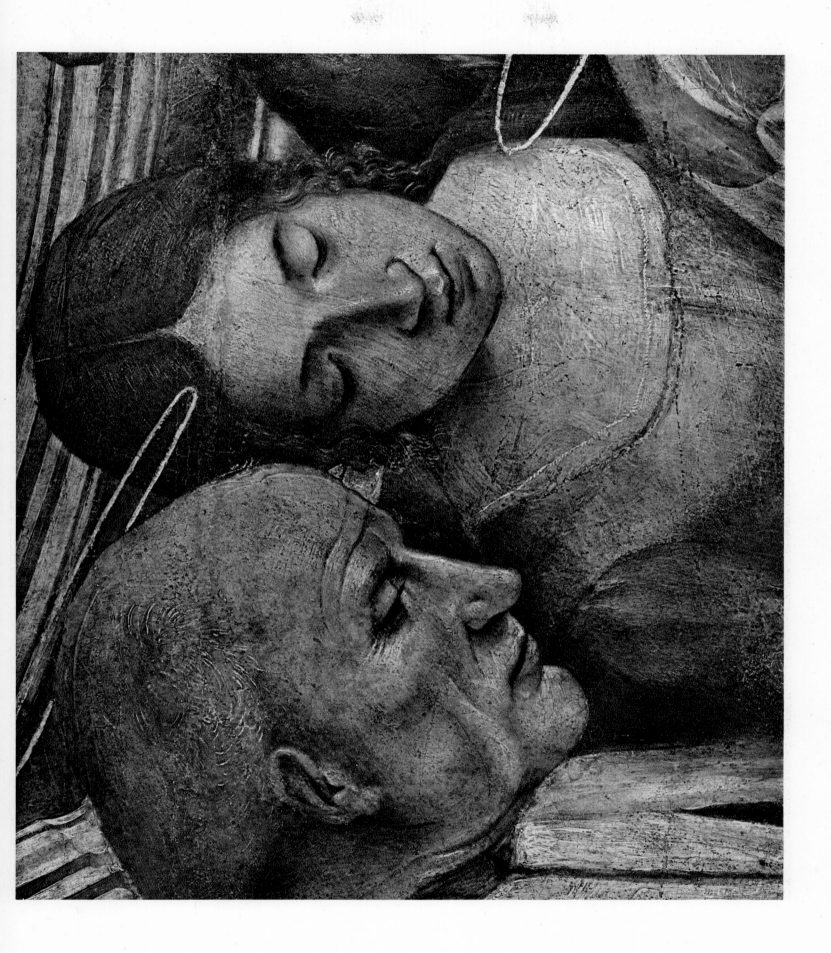